BLUE MOON OF KENTUCKY

A JOURNEY INTO THE WORLD OF *BLUEGRASS* AND *COUNTRY MUSIC* AS SEEN THROUGH THE CAMERA LENS OF PHOTO-JOURNALIST

LES LEVERETT

All of the photos in the first section of this book are in the permanent collection of the International Bluegrass Music Association Museum located in Owensboro, Kentucky, and at the time of this printing are displayed in the museum as a "one-man show."

PUBLISHED BY
EMPIRE PUBLISHING, INC.
PO BOX 717
MADISON, NC 27025-0717
PHONE 336-427-5850

Empire Publishing, Inc.
Box 717
Madison, NC 27025-0717
(336) 427-5850

Blue Moon of Kentucky © 1996 by Les Leverett

Library of Congress Catalog Number 96-86528
ISBN Number 0-944019-23-4

Published and printed in the United States of America

First Printing: 1996
Second Printing: 1999
1 2 3 4 5 6 7 8 9

COVER PHOTO: Lester Flatt and Earl Scruggs taping their Martha White* TV Show at WSM-TV Studios, May 20, 1964.
[Left to right]   Paul Warren, Earl Scruggs, "Uncle" Josh Graves, Lester Flatt, and "Cousin" Jake Tullock.

BACK COVER PHOTO by Libby Leverett-Crew

*Pet Milk co-sponsored the show.

For Emily Botein,
with best wishes & thanks!
Les Tenerett
May 2007

DEDICATION

For Dot, who was along on my journey, every step of the way; and to my children, John, Gary, and Libby, who have developed the same love for the music and respect for the musicians that I have.

Just prior to this book going into the final stages of printing, Bill Monroe, the creator of bluegrass music, passed from this life on the 9th day of September, in the year of our Lord, 1996. With respect and admiration, this page is dedicated to his memory.

William Smith "Bill" Monroe
The Father of Bluegrass Music
(September 13, 1911 - September 9, 1996)

A WORD FROM THE PUBLISHER

When you have been a professional photographer for most of your adult life and have shot thousands upon thousands of photographs in all, the question will be asked in conversation, "What are your favorite pictures you have taken through the years?" Now that is a very tough question to answer. Many of the photo shots are completely forgotten, erased from the mind entirely.

So when you get the go-ahead to compile a book that contains the photos that you wish to represent your life's work, which ones do you choose? After all, we're talking about a total of around 75 photographs that represent your life's work. How do you do that? Well, in discussion with Les, it was his decision which photos would be included in this project. It must be stated here that it was never his intention to exclude a particular person, performer, etc. Nor was there ever an attempt to cram as many bluegrass and/or country music stars into the book as possible. In choosing the photos, some were chosen because of their uniqueness — camera angles, special lighting situations, rareness (Patsy Cline & Governor Jimmie Davis in one shot, Lester Flatt, Earl Scruggs and band members on stools in cafe while on the road), etc. Some were selected because they bring back fond memories to the author & the principals involved. Many were chosen for their old-time presentation value.

In looking through this book you may quickly realize that some of your favorite entertainers may not be contained within. You may find some in photo lay-out that you may not think are justified in being here. Also, some subjects are used more than once — as in the case of Lester & Earl and Bill Monroe. Again, the author was not attempting to play the favorites game. In a nutshell, each and every photograph that this book contains represents the very best photographs taken by photographer Les Leverett of the bluegrass and country music artists.

Enjoy!

INTRODUCTION

Over the years, Les Leverett has earned the reputation as Nashville's premier music photographer, and has shot everything from record album covers to scenes of the Opry backstage. His photo archives are among the most extensive in the business, and his clients range from *Life* Magazine to The Nashville Network, from *American Heritage* to The Grand Ole Opry. Ever since the days when his office was in the old National Life building and he stood outside the window of WSM's Studio B to watch Lester and Earl sell Martha White flour, Les has had a special place in his heart for bluegrass music. His sense of history, passion for bluegrass, and his consummate skill with a camera made it only natural that he be honored with an exhibit by the International Bluegrass Music Museum.

It was my privilege to assist Les in choosing what we both considered to be the outstanding photographs that were to become part of the museum display, and ultimately, part of this book. At first, the prospect of going through the literally thousands of negatives, proofs, and images in Les's collection was daunting to both Les and myself. Then Les hit upon the idea of making a list of the bluegrass artists he had documented over the years, and then going through their files. There were few performers from 1960 to the present that weren't on this list; though Les was based in Nashville and for 32 years was the official Grand Ole Opry photographer. Most major bluegrass stars eventually came through Nashville, either as guests at Fan Fair or various Opry birthday celebrations, or as performers at local clubs.

As we looked through stacks and stacks of negatives, Les began to see many pictures that he had liked at the time he shot them but which he never had the opportunity to use. As a commercial photographer, he seldom got the chance to express his own preference for the photos which were published; for this exhibit, he has. There are many "first editions" here, as well as other images that will be familiar. We tried to avoid using too many pictures of bands performing in front of microphones. Les knows better than anyone else that this is only part of the bluegrass scene, and that shots made behind the scenes — backstage, at festivals, at recording or radio sessions, eating at roadside restaurants, or talking with fans — are as revealing as the more glamorous ones.

Students of motion pictures speak of the *auteur*—the artist who is able to work within the commercial industry and at the same time express his own imagination and vision. There is no better way to define the work of a man whose vision has for over three decades enhanced the dignity and beauty of bluegrass music—Les Leverett.

—Charles K. Wolfe

DR. CHARLES WOLFE

A Missouri native, Charles Wolfe has lived in the Nashville area for twenty-five years, and has written sixteen books and numerous articles on country music, folk music, and blues. He has annotated or produced over 100 albums and CDs, and has been three times nominated for Grammy awards. Among Dr. Wolfe's books are *Tennessee Strings, Kentucky Country,* biographies of Hall of Famer Grandpa Jones, black country star DeFord Bailey, and (with Kip Lornell) *The Life and Legend of Leadbelly,* a biography of the famous blues singer.

Wolfe is currently completing *The Music of Bill Monroe,* as well as a collection of Tennessee folk songs. In 1994 he did annotations for Bear Family's complete reissue of Bill Monroe's works. He continues to write and teach at Middle Tennessee State University near Nashville.

ACKNOWLEDGMENTS

A sincere thanks to those who identified people in photographs, and offered other valuable information: Dr. Perry Harris, Bill Harrison, John Hartford, Don Key, Lance Leroy, Jimmy Martin, Alan O"Bryant, Jim Scancarelli, Dallas Smith, Traci Todd, and Dr. Charles Wolfe.

—*Les Leverett*

Jam Session, Bean Blossom, Indiana, June 1970

This was shot under the canopy of an RV. That's Howdy Forrester and Doc Harris (who later founded the Grand Master's Fiddling Contest) looking on. I love the grouping; when I saw Doc and Howdy and the rest, I had to get interested.

The fiddler wearing the hat is Tommy Jarrell; Jimmy Arnold is on banjo. Kenny Baker is on the right; he was Monroe's fiddler at the time. Man with dark glasses and tie is fiddler Joe Green.

Jim and Jesse, Bean Blossom, Indiana, June 1970

Jim and Jesse are long-time friends of mine. I've done a lot of album cover work and studio portraits for them. Here, they had just finished their show and come off stage to meet with some fans.

Lester Flatt and Earl Scruggs Reading Mail, August 25, 1961

In a little over a week or so, I made two road trips with Flatt and Scruggs while a television documentary program about them was done, featuring Frank McGee. NBC had decided to do a piece on Lester and Earl out on the road for a show called *Here and Now,* and I was along to do some publicity photos for it. One of the trips was to a high school in Jumpertown, Mississippi, and on the bus on the way, Lester and Earl caught up on reading their mail. The show aired September 8, 1961.

The Whites, June 16, 1985

Many acts entertain between fiddlers competing, or while judges are doing their work, at The Grand Masters Fiddling Contest, held in the Gaslight Theatre at Opryland every June. That's when The Whites were captured in this shot. What a wonderful bunch! [Left to right] Buck White; daughters Rosie, Sharon (Mrs. Ricky Skaggs), and Cheryl; Jerry Douglas on dobro.

Sam Bush and Roy Acuff, April 1972

The first time they held the Grand Masters Fiddling Contest at Fan Fair, a lot of the events were in a big tent at Opryland, about where the Opry Museum is now. I hardly knew who Sam Bush was at the time, though I knew his father Charlie, a good friend of Roy's. I thought it was pretty unique — here's a guy with a headband and long hair — exactly the opposite of Roy Acuff's idea of a respectable image. Roy didn't like that long hair, yet he was extremely friendly to Sam, perhaps because he knew his daddy. In the background, Ebo Walker and "Junior" Curtis Burch.

Reno and Smiley, October 1971

We didn't know it at the time, but Red Smiley had only a few weeks left when I caught him with Don Reno on stage at the old Ryman at the Opry Birthday Celebration. I'd heard of these two for so long and was thrilled to finally be able to see and hear them doing their music in person. Their fiddler is Buck Ryan.

Bill Monroe, June 1982

I was out at Monroe's farm, shooting for ABC Radio's *American Country Countdown* ad campaign, doing a series of pictures for "Carrying the Tradition Forward," where we paired younger with older artists — in this case Ricky Skaggs and Bill Monroe. After we finished shooting the pictures, Bill wanted us to see his place, so we went walking around the barns.

McLain Family Band, June 1975

This was Fan Fair 1975, at the Opry House. I don't recall when I first heard this band, but I was really impressed with them. Here they had just returned from one of their European tours. I later came to know the two girls and Raymond. [Left to right] Raymond W. McLain, banjo; Alice, mandolin; Ruth, bass; and father, Raymond K. McLain.

RV Campers and Pickers, Bean Blossom, Indiana, June 1970

This is one of many groups that were cooking and eating lunch while taking a break from the picking and singing.

Flatt and Scruggs, Roadside Cafe, August 1961

On the way down to Jumpertown, Mississippi, the Flatt and Scruggs bus stopped at a little roadside cafe to eat lunch. It was better than that night's supper, I remember. That night, "Cousin" Jake Tullock, "Uncle" Josh Graves, and I went into a little grocery store just a few steps from the high school and got cans of Vienna sausages. We stood out by the back steps of the school and ate those for supper. Bluegrass musicians don't always eat right; it's a wonder they don't all die from insufficient diets. [Left to right] Flatt & Scruggs fiddler Paul Warren, Lester Flatt, Curly Seckler, and Earl Scruggs.

Bill Monroe's Mandolin, January 26, 1974

This close-up of Bill Monroe's hands was taken while rehearsing and playing in his dressing room at the old Ryman. It was less than two months before the Opry moved to the new Opry House at Opryland.

Ralph Stanley, October 1973

This was at the Ryman during the Early Bird Bluegrass concert at the Opry's 48th Birthday Celebration. When Ralph Stanley's band was on stage, I always managed to be near. Ricky Lee and the late Roy Lee Centers on guitars.

Lester Flatt, July 1969

I was out at WSM one morning while Lester was doing a radio show with the Nashville Grass, and I decided to pop a shot or two. The show was over and Lester was starting to put his guitar away, when I asked him to just stop a minute so I could get this shot. It's such a natural picture of him; I don't think it's ever been in print before.

Ralph Stanley with Ricky Skaggs, October 1971

It's a little bit strange, but I love this picture. This is the first time it's ever been printed. It is a picture of Ralph and his group performing. Ricky Skaggs was with the group at the time. Years later, when I heard Ricky talk about being with Ralph, I started going through old negatives and this is the only one I found that included Ricky. It is so doggone different because Ralph has turned and is staring at me like he thinks I'm going to slip in and start singing bass or something. I had a telephoto lens and was back a lot further than you might think I was. This was at the Ryman Auditorium, then the Grand Old Opry House, during Bill Monroe's Early Bird Bluegrass Show, a part of the Opry's 46th Birthday Celebration. [Left to right] Jack Cooke, Keith Whitley, Ralph Stanley, Curly Ray Cline, Ricky Skaggs.

Mac Wiseman, June 1978

It is impossible to take a bad picture of Mac Wiseman because his countenance is always so warm and friendly. He's always smiling. I like this one because it is a nice close-up and you can see that beard and mustache, those hairs shining in the side light. That's Alan O'Bryant on the right.

Jimmy Martin, October 1971

I just happen to love this picture. It shows Jimmy off really well. To me, Jimmy is one of the best singers in bluegrass music. I came to know Jimmy pretty early in my music business career. I remember him having a song titled "I Can't Quit Cigarettes," and we made a gag shot of him with a mouth full of cigarettes and an ashtray full of butts and matches. On banjo, Tim Spradlin; mandolin, Darrel Samson; bass, Sheridon Samson; snare, Jimmy Martin, Jr.

Bill Monroe's Mandolin Case, January 4, 1975

Bill's mandolin case sits next to a jar of pickles somebody brought to him, an Opryland coffee cup, and has some fan letters underneath. I can't imagine why the Johnny Rodriguez sticker is on the case, unless Johnny just did it, or maybe Bill just said, "I kind of like you, boy," and stuck it down there himself. Who knows?

Doc Watson, January 10, 1975

Bill Littleton, who wrote for *Performance Magazine,* asked me to go with him one night to the Exit-Inn in Nashville, to see Doc and Merle Watson. He had an interview set up with Doc. It thrilled me, because I had never actually met Doc before. There was an old trailer that sat out back of the Exit-Inn which served as a sort of dressing room where we went with Doc. I shot this during the interview; I don't think it has ever been seen before.

Flatt and Scruggs on the Air, June 5, 1963

When Lester and Earl had that early morning Martha White show, they would cut a whole bunch of them at one time up on the fifth floor, in Studio B of WSM, in the old National Life building. What was amazing was how they would know exactly what they were going to do next — they never had to stop the tape and go back. They worked that microphone like ballet dancers, in and out, and I could not pass by that studio without stopping and watching for a few minutes. You could hear 'em all up and down the hall when they were cutting; you could *feel* them in there. [Left to right] Paul Warren, fiddler; Earl Scruggs, "Cousin" Jake Tullock, bass; Lester Flatt.

Bean Blossom, Indiana, Countryside, June 1970

Bill had always wanted me to come up to his festival, so my wife, daughter and I did one June. We had to park quite a distance away, but because of that we got to see all of those parking lot pickers. One of the fans we ran into that day was Bud Wendell, the Grand Ole Opry manager. Bud has been one of Bill Monroe's biggest fans all these years. He is now President and CEO of Gaylord Entertainment Company, which owns the Grand Ole Opry, Opryland, TNN, etc.

Bluegrass Cardinals, June 1982

This was from the Fan Fair bluegrass concert at the Nashville fairgrounds. What harmony! Photography on this show was always difficult because of the bright afternoon sky behind the stage. [Left to right] Tim Smith, Norman Wright, John Davis, David Parmley, Don Parmley.

Bill Monroe with Dancers, Fan Fair, June 1978.

It's always a kick to see Bill Monroe dance; every once in a while he gets so carried away with all the music, he just can't help himself. When the cloggers come out there, he has to go and help them a little bit. Here he was just momentarily having a time with one of the dancing girls. The fiddlers are James Bryan and Kenny Baker.

Johnson Mountain Boys, October 1983

This was a later Opry Birthday Celebration, and the Johnson Mountain Boys were doing the Early Bird Bluegrass Show — their first time to appear on the Opry stage. Man alive, they're really something! [Left to right] David McLaughlin, Richard Underwood, Dudley Connell, Larry Robbin, Eddie Stubbs.

Jim and Jesse with Lester Flatt, 1972

They were taping a pilot at WSM-TV for a new series called *Bluegrass Express* that they were hoping to syndicate. Apparently it never sold, but they had some good people on the program that night. [In the background, left to right] Paul Warren, Roland White, and Johnny Johnson on bass.

The Boys from Shiloh, October 1988

Bobby Smith passed away a few years ago. I hated to hear that because I really liked those fellows' music, and I knew of his love for music. Included in photo are Wayne Jeralds on fiddle, Brian Fesler on banjo, Doyle Nikirk on mandolin, and brothers Kenneth Smith, Dallas Smith, and the late Bobby Smith.

Bill Monroe, Bean Blossom, Indiana, June 1970

I was hanging out in back of the stage area, when my eye caught movement at the bottom of the small hill there. It turned out to be Bill Monroe taking a little walk. As he topped the crest of the hill, he paused for several seconds to survey the situation. I have no way of knowing what his thoughts were, but he looked so alone at that moment.

The Lewis Family, October 1974

It's awfully hard to get a shot of this bunch where you can see all of them doing their act. I always loved to watch them; they are such a visual as well as a "listening to" group. [Left to right] Miggie, Polly, Pop, Janis, Little Roy, and Wallace. This was shot at The Bluegrass Concert during the Opry's 49th Birthday Celebration at the Grand Ole Opry House.

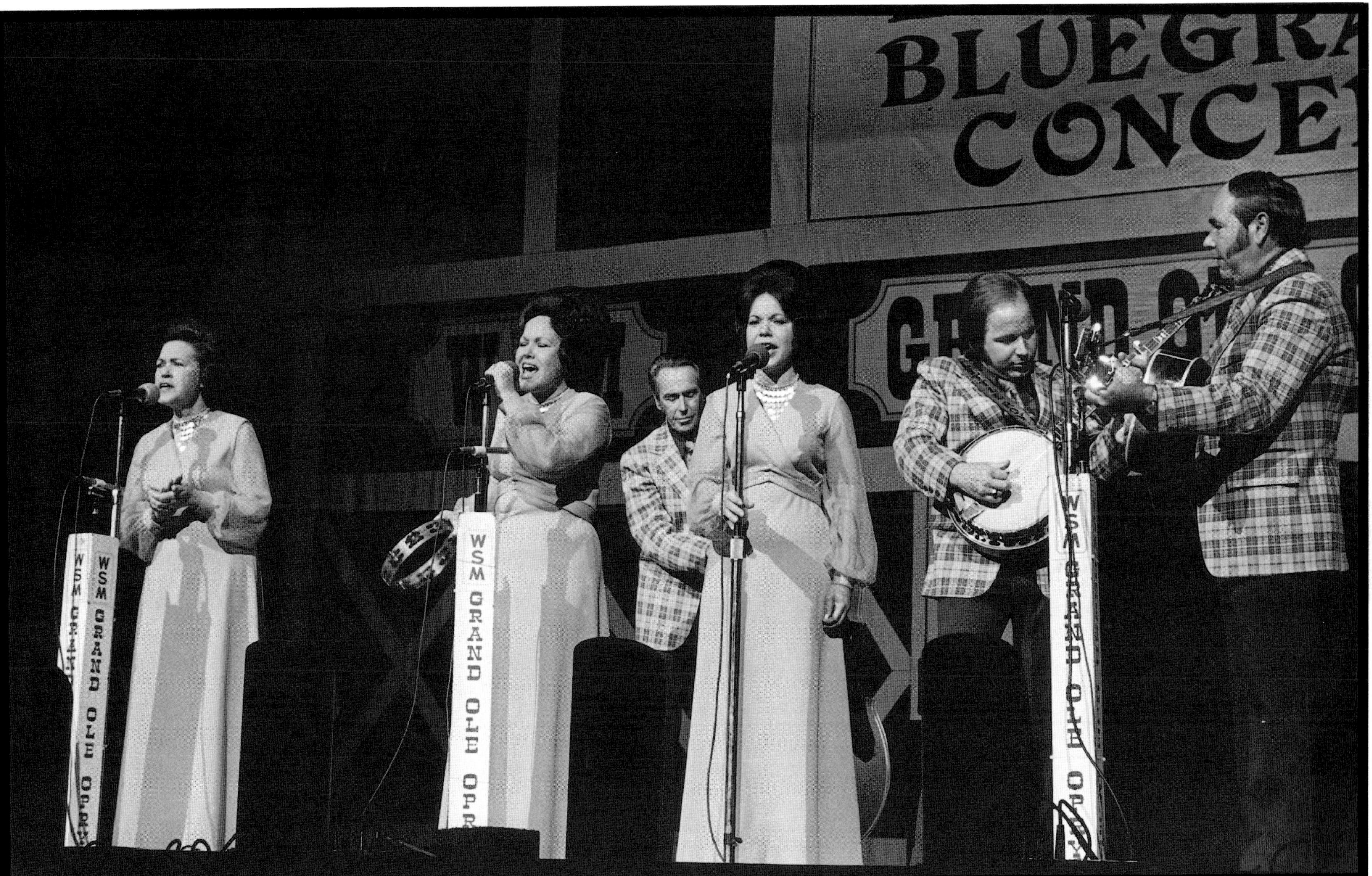
BLUEGRA
CONCE
WSM GRAND OLE OPR

Hubert Davis, October 1974

This is another picture from the 49th Opry Birthday Celebration; I always did admire and like Hubert. It was part of my job then to shoot all the acts, and I always felt this was a good picture of him and his group. [Left to right] Richard Hoffman, Gene Bush, Hubert Davis, wife, Ruby, and Shelby Jean Davis.

The Osbornes and Lester Flatt, February 14, 1976

I have no idea why the Osbornes (Bobby, center, Sonny playing banjo) and Lester Flatt's group were on the same Opry segment, but they were. At one point during that show, they got together and just tore the audience up. Marty Stuart (left of microphone) was a member of Lester's group at the time. That's Lester's fiddler, Paul Warren on left. (Flatt & Scruggs had split at this time. Lester's group was The Nashville Grass.)

Bill Monroe and Colonel Sanders, May 1966

Colonel Sanders, the founder of Kentucky Fried Chicken, appeared at the Opry one night for some unknown or "unremembered" reason. The Colonel knew who Bill Monroe was and posed for a picture. I like the idea of having together two men who had created two of Kentucky's best known products.

[Left] **Alison Krauss, May 1991**

This was at the Opry, pretty stark, with her in the spotlight, a lot of shadow. That fiddle bow's a'humming, and every hum right on key. What a great talent!

[Right] **Earl Scruggs, October 1965**

There was a bench by the announcer's stand on the Opry stage at the Ryman, and one night I happened to be sitting there next to Earl while he was waiting to go on. I saw that Martha White backdrop behind him with his profile to the audience and I just reached over and made this picture. This is another picture that has never been used anywhere before.

[Left] **Dad Sullivan, June 1978**

I have many shots of the Sullivan Family playing, but this particular picture was taken at a Fan Fair held at the Municipal Auditorium in downtown Nashville. I was coming from backstage and, as I was walking by those canvas drops, I happened to look over, and way down at the end, at the back of the stage, was Dad Sullivan looking around those metal folding chairs, watching whoever was performing. I don't think he even knew I shot it.

[Right] **Vassar Clements, May 1977**

My friend Bill Littleton was doing a story for *Performance Magazine* and asked me to go with him to the Pickin' Parlor (in Nashville) to shoot a picture they could use. Backstage, where they repaired instruments, we talked to Vassar. I had admired Vassar but had never met him. I shot some pictues of him performing, and after he worked up a sweat — which wasn't hard to do in that little place — I got this picture.

[Left] Bill Monroe and Doc Watson, June 1970

This photo was shot on the steps behind the stage at Bean Blossom, Indiana. Bill and Doc were just talking and enjoying being together.

[Right] John Hartford, June 1994

When the renovation of the old Ryman was finished, there was a dedication ceremony and a lot of people from the music community were there walking around and looking her over. I was walking by those old stained glass windows and there was John Hartford inspecting the place. He looked so great just standing there with the early morning light pouring in that window; he looked like he *belonged* there.

[Left] Ricky Skaggs, May 15, 1982

This was the night the Opry announced that Ricky was becoming a full-fledged member of the cast. He was rehearsing in the dressing room with his band. On the left is Bobby Hicks; on right, "Hoot" Hester.

[Right] Curly Ray Cline, June 1988

I always loved to watch Curly Ray work — the way he'd get out there and twist and get after that fiddle. I had quit shooting the Fan Fair formally, but my daughter Libby was working it, so I went along to the fairgrounds to shoot some of the acts just for fun. Curly was on stage with Ralph Stanley, of course.

[Left] Reno and Harrell, October 1972

Another nice grouping from an Early Bird Bluegrass show. I think Bill Harrell is one of the best singers in the business, and I've always loved Don Reno. The epitome of good bluegrass picking and singing.

[Right] Wilma Lee Cooper, June 1982

Standing backstage at Fan Fair, Wilma Lee was checking to see if her guitar was in tune. There was no plan; she just happened to be there, and it looked good to me. I've always loved Wilma Lee, and her late husband and partner, Stoney. In the background is Terry Smith, her bass player.

[Left] Joe Stuart, October 1975

This was from the bluegrass show at the 50th anniversary of the Opry. I had enjoyed hearing Joe on so many of Bill Monroe's records, and was so, so sorry to lose that man.

[Right] Kenny Baker, June 7, 1974

This was from the first Early Bird Bluegrass Concert held at the *new* Opry House. I've always liked Kenny's playing so much, and I like Kenny as a person, and when you like somebody, you look for ways to make them look good in a photograph. I love to shoot from behind, looking toward the spotlight to get the silhouette. Though you don't see faces, it's a graphic, pictorial thing. So there was Kenny just sawing away and I got back there and focused on him and waited for his head to turn to see a little bit of his face.

[Left] Alan O'Bryant and the Smith Brothers, October 31, 1974

Hazel Smith, a long-time columnist for *Country Music* magazine as well as a songwriter for Bill Monroe and others, is the mother of Billy and Terry Smith. At the time this picture was taken they had not been in town long and she wanted to help them get a start. She asked me to shoot some pictures, so we went out to Shelby Park in Nashville in order to get a decent background without a lot of power lines and cars and houses. Alan, right, was age 18. Billy, left, was 17, and Terry, on bass, was 14. The other young man in the picture is Mike Hartgrove, now with Third Tyme Out. Terry now plays bass with the Osborne Brothers, and of course, Alan is with the Nashville Bluegrass Band.

[Right] Emmylou Harris and Grandpa Jones, January 15, 1983

Another one of the pairings for *American Country Countdown's* "Carrying the Tradition Forward" series. This shot was taken at a studio in Nashville where Emmylou was recording. Grandpa met me there and we had to wait for her to finish. They're going through some old songs Grandpa liked. . . the young picking up some of the old treasures.

Section II
MORE OF LES'S FAVORITES

Originally, it was the author's concept to feature in this book only the photos on display at the International Bluegrass Music Museum. These are featured in the first section. Just prior to finalizing the book, the decision was made to include some additional photos of country and bluegrass musicians.

The following pages contain more photographs that are very special to photographer Les Leverett. We were delighted to add the following photos to this publication. We simply call this added section "More of Les's Favorites."

Opry Stars, October 7, 1961

Some of the Opry ladies gathered in a shot backstage at the Opry: Minnie Pearl, Wilma Lee Cooper, Jan Howard, Skeeter Davis, June Carter, and Kitty Wells.

Owen Bradley and Conway Twitty, November 2, 1965

Decca A&R man, Owen Bradley, and Conway Twitty at a recording session being done at the "Quonset Hut," where many great recordings were made.

Roy Acuff's Dressing Room, Opry House, July 12, 1980

Opry member Boxcar Willie sings along with Jon Walmsley, ("Jason" on "The Waltons" television program). Jon was visiting the Opry.

On the "Hee Haw" Set, October 15, 1982

George "Goober" Lindsey, Archie Campbell, Grandpa Jones, Merle Travis, Junior Samples, Lulu Roman, and Roy Acuff.

Opry Stars Johnny Russell and the Late Del Wood, February 15, 1983

This photo was taken at a private party. I accused Del of sitting next to Johnny in order to make herself appear smaller, since she had been on a diet. It seemed to work for her, anyway.

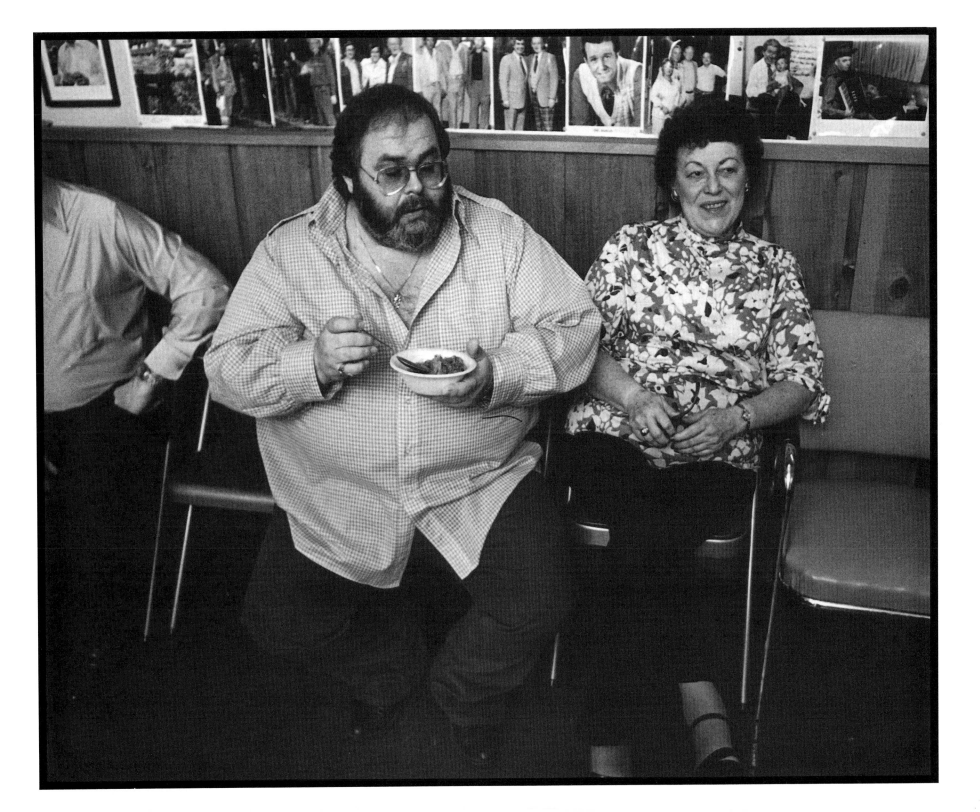

Backstage Hoedown, Fan Fair, June 11, 1977 Reunion Show

These folks were having a great time when I came across them in Nashville's Municipal Auditorium . . . and so did I. Pictured are Eleanor Parker, Martha Carson, Joe Maphis, Merle Travis, Rose Lee Maphis, Biff Collie, Rex Parker, Kenny Roberts, and Buddy Durham. This was after they had all appeared on the Reunion Show.

Columbia Studio (Quonset Hut), November 11, 1964

Grady Martin and Pete Drake (on steel guitar) flank Carl and Pearl Butler at their recording session.

Roy Acuff's Dressing Room, February 17, 1979

Minnie Pearl breaks 'em up with a funny story in Roy Acuff's dressing room. Listening also are Opry stars Jeanne Pruett, and the late Ben Smathers, leader of the Stoney Mountain Cloggers.

Louie Armstrong and Johnny Cash, October 5, 1970

This was shot during the taping of Johnny Cash's ABC-TV Show in the Ryman Auditorium.

Hank Thompson, Kitty Wells, and Johnny Wright (Kitty's husband), October 12, 1981

These three posed for my camera at a reception held in the Opryland Hotel, following the CMA Awards Show.

Porter Wagoner and the Wagonmasters, April 1969

This was shot at a recording session at RCA Studios. George McCormick on guitar, Mac Magaha on fiddle, and Buck Trent on banjo.

Hank Snow and Cindy Walker, December 25, 1971

Cindy has composed many songs for a variety of country and western stars. Here she is seen backstage at the Opry in the old Ryman Auditorium. (I wonder if she sold Hank the song?)

Carl Butler, Stu Phillips and Ernest Tubb, September 11, 1971

These three catch up on their visitation in one of the Opry dressing rooms at the Ryman.

Lonzo (Dave Wooten), Doug Kershaw, and Oscar Sullivan, June 14, 1969

Kershaw visits Wooten and Sullivan in their dressing room backstage at the Opry.

The Stoney Mountain Cloggers, February 23, 1974

Ben and Margaret Smathers, center, daughter Candy, left, sons Mickey and Hal, right, of the The Stoney Mountain Cloggers, dance at the Opry. I've always loved this shot, because daughter Debbie is seen with only one leg, which makes her mother appear to have three legs.

Gordon Terry, Merle Haggard, and Johnny Gimble, October 1977

Three great fiddlers entertain during the Opry's 52nd Birthday Celebration.

Jammin' at Grandpa's, 1989

John Hartford and Ramona Jones fiddled together at a get-together at Grandpa and Ramona Jones' home. Frazier Moss is playing his fiddle in the background.

Sid Harkreader, June 13, 1981

Sid Harkreader, one of the first fiddlers on the real early days of the Grand Ole Opry, was caught by my camera backstage during the Reunion Show at Fan Fair. The event was held in Nashville's Municipal Auditorium.

Hank Snow and Porter Wagoner, Backstage at the Opry, January 5, 1974

Porter is showing Hank Snow the composite I had done on January 2nd for a proposed album cover. It was finally used with the title "Highway Headed South."

Johnny Cash on the Ryman Stage, May 12, 1972

Johnny Cash, as he appeared on Jimmie Rodger Snow's "Grand Ole Gospel Show." I knew that if I shot with that spotlight barely creeping into the top edge of my view-finder, with the wide angle lens, I could get a "halo" effect, which, considering the spiritual song that Johnny was singing, seemed appropriate.

[Left] Loretta Lynn and George Burns, September 18, 1980

When I caught these two in the Opry House Lounge during the taping of Burns' TV special, Loretta stopped me to tell Burns about our long friendship. A local photographer was setting the two up for a shot, and I, actually, was an intruder. Loretta talked to George so much about me being the first photographer in Nashville to shoot her picture that the other photographer said, "Okay, Loretta, *now* let *me* shoot your picture."

[Right] "Woody" Paul of The Riders in the Sky, December 11, 1982

"Woody" Paul (Chrisman) was practicing his lasso twirling in the hallway at the Grand Ole Opry House when I came upon the scene.

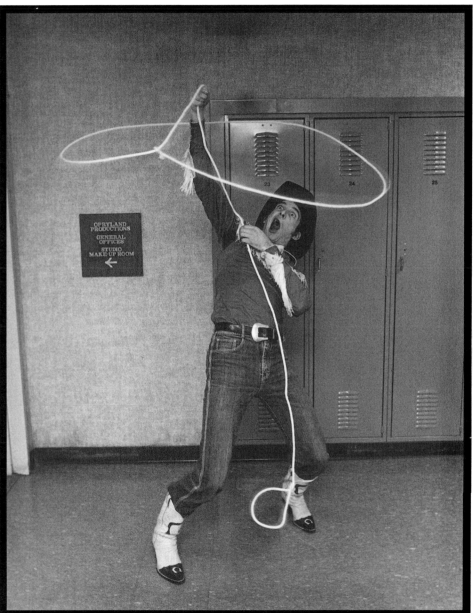

[Left] Roy Acuff, in His Opry House Dressing Room, August 11, 1979

Roy is practicing his yo-yo throwing to the pleasure of all. To the left are Jimmy Riddle and Onie Wheeler, both long-time members of Roy's Smokey Mountain Boys. All three are gone now, and I miss them a lot. To the right is friend H. G. Roberts.

[Right] "Governor" Jimmie Davis and Patsy Cline, November 3, 1961

The former governor of Louisiana, Jimmie Davis, and Patsy Cline visit at the WSM Breakfast at the Grand Ole Opry Birthday Celebration.

[Left] **Maybelle Carter, February 12, 1970**

Mother Maybelle, of the original Carter Family, plays autoharp and sings on son-in-law Johnny Cash's ABC-TV Show, taped at the Grand Ole Opry House (Ryman Auditorium).

[Right] **Little Jimmy Dickens and Jean Shepard, January 8, 1983**

I don't remember the reason Jean Shepard was holding the mike for Little Jimmy Dickens, but these are two of my all-time favorite country singers.

[Left] June Carter, March 26, 1962

June has just kicked off her right shoe out toward the audience, as part of her act. I picked it up and held it (too long to suit June) before giving it back. Frances Lyle is picking on the right.

[Right] Gene Autry at CMA Awards Show, October 1969

Upon being named to the CMA Hall of Fame, Autry said, "I don't deserve this, but then, I have arthritis, and I don't deserve that either." Tennessee Ernie Ford and Tex Ritter presented the award to Autry and are seen behind him. In the background: Bobby Goldsboro, Jeannie C. Riley, and Ed McMahon, who was also a presenter that night.

[Left] Bashful Brother Oswald, March 1974

Bashful Brother Oswald (Pete Kirby), long time member of Roy Acuff's Smokey Mountain Boys, is waiting to "go on."

[Right] Tex Ritter, August 11, 1973

I came upon Tex Ritter backstage at the Opry leaning on this old amplifier, and with this very pensive look on his face. He had less than five months to live at the time.

Other Books Available from Empire Publishing:

1001 Toughest TV Trivia Questions of All Time by Vincent Terrace
Allan "Rocky" Lane, Republic's Action Ace by Chuck Thornton and David Rothel
The Allied Artists Checklist by Len D. Martin
America on the Rerun by David Story
An Ambush of Ghosts by David Rothel
Award Winning Films by Peter C. Mowrey
Best of Universal by Tony Thomas
Betty Grable: The Girl with the Million Dollar Legs by Tom McGee
The Beverly Hillbillies
Black Hollywood by Gary Null
Black Hollywood: From 1960 to Today by Gary Null
The Brady Bunch Book by Andrew J. Eledstein and Frank Lovece
Bugsy by James Toback
B-Western Actors Encyclopedia by Ted Holland
Candid Cowboys, Vols. 1 & 2 by Neil Summers
Cartoon Movie Posters by Bruce Hershenson
Charlie Chan and the Movies by Ken Hanke
The "Cheers" Trivia Book by Mark Wenger
Child Star by Chirley Temple Black
Classic TV Westerns by Ronald Jackson
Classics of the Gangster Film by Robert Bookbinder
Classics of the Horror Film by Williams K. Everson
C'mon Get Happy by David Cassidy
The Columbia Checklist by Len D. Martin
Complete Films of Audrey Hepburn
Complete Films of Bela Lugosi by Richard Bojarski
Complete Films of Bette Davis by Gene Ringgold
Complete Films of Cary Grant by Donald Deschner
Complete Films of Cecil B. DeMille by Gene Ringgold and DeWitt Bodeen
Complete Films of Charlie Chaplin by Gerald D. McDonald
Complete Films of Clark Gable by Gabe Essoe
Complete Films of Edward G. Robinson by Alvin H. Marill
Complete Films of Erroll Flynn by Tony Thomas, et al
Complete Films of Frank Capra by Victor Scherle & William Turner Levy
Complete Films of Gary Cooper by Homer Dickens
Complete Films of Henry Fonda by Tony Thomas
Complete Films of Ingrid Bergman by Lawrence J. Quirk
Complete Films of James Cagney by Homer C. Dickens
Complete Films of Jeanette MacDonald and Nelson Eddy by Philip Castanza
Complete Films of Joan Crawford by Lawrence J. Quirk
Complete Films of John Huston by John McCarty
Complete Films of John Wayne by Mark Ricci, et al
Complete Films of Judy Garland by Joe Morella and Edward Z Epstein
Complete Films of Laurel & Hardy by William K. Everson
Complete Films of Mae West by Jon Tuska
Complete Films of Marilyn Monroe by Michael Conway and Mark Ricci
Complete Films of Marlene Dietrich by Homer Dickens
Complete Films of the Marx Brothers by Allen Eyles
Complete Films of Orson Wells by James Howard
Complete Films of Rita Hayworth by Gene Ringgold
Complete Films of Spencer Tracy by Donald Deschner
Complete Films of Steve McQueen by Casey St. Chamez
Complete Films of W. C. Fields by Donald Deschner
Complete Films of William Holden by Lawrence J. Quirk
Complete Films of William Powell by Lawrence J. Quirk
Country Sunshine by Judy Berryhill and Frances Meeker
Cowboy Movie Posters by Bruce Hershenson
The Cowboy and the Kid by J. Brim Crow III and Jack H. Smith
Cult Horror Films by Everman
Curly by Joan Howard Maurer

The Cutting Room Floor by Laurent Bouzereau
A Darling of the Twenties: Madge Bellamy
Dave's World The Dick Powell Story by Tony Thomas
Dick Tracy: America's Most Famous Detective edited by Bill Crouch, Jr.
Divine Images by Roy Kinnard and Tim Davis
Don Miller's Hollwood Corral by Smith & Hulse
Early Classics of the Foreign Film by Parker Tyler
Elvis: A Celebration in Pictures by Charles Hirshbergh and the editors of *Life Magazine*
The Essential Hank Williams by Tim Jones
Evenings with Cary Grant by Nance Nelson
Everybody on the Truck: The Story of the Dillards by Lee Grant with the Original Dillards
Famous Hollywood Locations by Leon Smith
Fantastic Cinema Subject Guide
Favorite Families of TV
Feature Players: The Stories Behind the Faces, Vol. 2 by Jim & Tom Goldrup
The Film Encyclopedia
Film Flubs by Bill Givens
Films and Career of Elvis by Steven Zmijewsky and Boris Zmijewski
Film Flubs, The Sequal by Bill Givens
Films and Career of Audie Murphy by Sue Gossett
Films of Alfred Hitchcock by Robert A. Harris and Michael S. Lasky
Films of Al Pacino by Schoell
Films of Arnold Schwarzenegger by John L. Flynn
Films of Carole Lombard by Fred W. Ott
Films of Clint Eastwood by Boris Zmijewsky and Lee Pfeiffer
Films of Dustin Hoffman by Douglas Brode
Films of Elizabeth Taylor by Jerry Vermilye and Aldo Vigano
Films of Federico Fellini by Claudio Fava & Aldo Vigano
Films of Frank Sinatra by Gene Ringgold and Clifford McCarty
Films of Gina Lollobrigida by Maurizio Ponzi
Films of Gloria Swanson by Lawrence J. Quirk
Films of Gregory Peck by John Griggs
Films of Greta Garbo by Conway et al
Films of Hopalong Cassidy by Francis M. Nevins, Jr.
Films of Jack Nicholson by Douglas Brode
Films of Jane Fonda by George Hadley-Garcia
Films of Katharine Hepburn by Homer Dickens
Films of Kirk Douglas by Tony Thomas
Films of Lauren Bacall by Lawrence J. Quirk
Films of Laurence Olivier by Margaret Morley
Films of Marlon Brando by Tony Thomas
Films of Merchant Ivory by Long
Films of Norma Shearer by Jack Jacobs and Myron Braum
Films of Olivia DeHavilland by Tony Thomas
Films of Paul Newman by Lawrence J. Quirk
Films of Peter Lorre by Stephen D. Youngkin, James Bigwood, and Raymond Cabana, Jr.
Films of Robert DeNiro by Douglas Brode
Films of Robert Redford by James Spada
Films of Sean Connery by Lee Pfeiffer and Phillip Lisa
Films of Shirley MacLaine by Christopher Paul Denis
Films of Shirley Temple by Robert Windeler
Films of Steven Spielberg by Douglas Brode
Films of the Eighties by Douglas Brode
Films of the Fifties by Douglas Brode
Films of the Seventies by Robert Bookbinder
Films of the Sixties by Douglas Brode
Films of the Thirties by Jerry Vermilye
Films of Warren Beatty by Lawrence Quirk
Films of Woody Allen by Douglas Brode
Final Curtain: Deaths of Noted Movie & TV Personalities

First Films by Jami Bernard
Frankly, My Dear by Bloch
From Bruce Lee to the Ninjas: Martial Arts Movies by Meyers
Garth Brooks Scrapbook by Lee Randall
Gene Autry Reference-Trivia-Scrapbook by David Rothel
Gene Roddenbery: The Myth and the Man by Joel Engel
Gilligan, Maynard and Me by Bob Denver
Grand National Producers Releasing Corporation and Screen Guild
Great Baseball Films by Rob Edelman
Great German Films by Frederick W. Ott
Great Italian Films by Jerry Vermilye
Great Radio Personalities by Anthony Slide
Great Science Fiction Films by Richard Meyers
Great War Films
Growing Up Brady by Barry Williams
Halliwell's Film Guide
Hello, I Must Be Going by Chandler
Here on Gilligan's Isle by Russell Johnson and Steve Cox
Hispanic Hollywood by George Hadley-Garcia
Hollywood Bedlam by William K. Everson
Hollywood Musical by Tony Thomas
Hollywood USA by Randal Patrick and Phil Kramer
Hollywood Western by William K. Everson
Hopalong Cassidy: The Clarence E. Mulford Story by Bernard A. Drew
Howard Hughes in Hollywood by Tony Thomas
How to Meet and Hang Out with the Stars
I Love Lucy: Complete Picture History by Michael McClay
In a Door, Into a Fight, Out a Door, Into a Chase by William Whitney
Incredible World of 007 by Lee Pfeiffer & Philip Lisa
Inside Mayberry by Dan Harrison and Bill Habeeb
In the Nick of Time: Motion Picture Sound Serials by William C. Cline
Jack Lemmon: His Films and Career by Joe Baltake
James Dean: Behind the Scene by Adams & Burns, ed.
James Dean: Little Boy Lost by Joe Hyams
Jewish Image in American Film by Lester D. Friedman
Jim Carrey Scrapbook by Scott & Barbara Siegel
Joel McCrea, Riding the High Country by Tony Thomas
John Wayne Scrapbook by Lee Pfeiffer
Judy Garland: The Secret Life of an American Legend by David Shipman
Keep Watching the Skies by Bill Warren
King Cowboy: Tom Mix and the Movies by Robert S. Birchard
Kings of the Jungle by David Fury
Life & Films of Buck Jones: The SIlent Era by Buck Rainey
Life & Films of Buck Jones: The Sound Era by Buck Rainey
Live Television by Frank Sturcken
Lon Chaney: The Man Behind the Thousand Faces by Michael F. Blake
Lost Films of the Fifties by Douglas Brode
Lucille: The Life of Lucille Ball by Kathleen Brady
Madonna Scrapbook by Lee Randall
Marilyn and Me: Sisters, Rivals, Friends by Susan Strasberg
Me 'n' Elvis by Charlie Hodge
Modern Horror Film by John McCarty
Moe Howard & the Three Stooges by Moe Howard
The Monogram Checklist by Ted Okuda
More Character People by Arthur F. McClure, Alfred E. Twomey, & Ken Jones
More Classics of the Horror Film by William K. Everson
More Cowboy Shooting Stars by John A. Rutherford and Richard B. Smith, III
Movie Psychos and Madmen by John McCarty
Muriel Ostriche: Princess of Silent Films by Q. David Bowers
Nightmare Never Ends: The Official History of Freddy Krueger by William Schoell

Northern Exposure Book: The Official Publication of the Television of the Television Series by Louis Chunovic
Northern Exposures by Rob Morrow
Official Andy Griffith Show Scrapbook by Lee Pfeiffer
The Official Dick Van Dyke Show by Vince Waldron
Official John Wayne Reference Book by Charles John Kieskalt
Official TV Western Book, Vols. 1, 2,3, & 4 by Neil Summers
Old Familiar Faces by Robert A. Juran
Partridge Family Album by Joey Green
Poverty Row Horrors by Tom Weaver
Randolph Scott / A Film Biography by Jefferson Brim Crow, III
The Real Bob Steele and a Man Called Brad by Bob Nareau
The Republic Chapterplays by R. M. Hayes
Republic Confidential: Volume2 - The Players by Jack Mathis
Riding the Video Range by Gary A. Yoggy
The RKO Features by James L. Neibaur
The Round-Up by Donald R. Key
Round Up the Usual Suspects by Aljean Harmetz
Roy Rogers by Robert W. Phlllips
Roy Rogers Reference-Trivia-Scrapbook by David Rothel
Saddle Gals by Edgar M. Wyatt and Steve Turner
Saddle Pals by Garv Towell and Wayne E. Keates
Saddle Serenaders by Guy Logsdon, Mary Rogers and William Jacobson
Second Feature by John Cocchi
Serials-ly Speaking by William C. Cline
The Shoot-em-Ups Ride Again by Buck Rainey
Silent Film Necrology by Eugene Michael Vazzana
Silent Portraits by Anthony Slide
Sinatra Scrapbook by Gary L. Doctor
Singing Cowboy Stars by Robert Phillips
Son of Film Flubs by Bill Givens
Speaking of Silents: First Ladies of the Screen by William Drew
Star Trek Movie Memories by William Shatner
Stroke of Fortune by William C. Cline
Sunday Nights at Seven: The Jack Benny Story by Jack Benny and his daughter Joan
Television Westerns by Richard West
They Sang! They Danced! They Romanced! by John Springer
They Still Call Me Junior by Frank "Junior" Coghlan
Those Fabulous Serial Heroines by Buck Rainey
Three Stooges Scrapbook by Jeff Lenburg, Joan Howard Maurer, Greg Lenburg
Thrillers: Seven Decades of Classic Film Suspense by John McCarthy
Tim Holt by David Rothel
Tom Mix: a Heavily-Illustrated Biography by Paul E. Mix
Tom Mix Book by M. G. "Bud" Norris
Tom Mix Highlights by Andy Woytowch
Tom Mix: The Formative Years by Paul E. Mix
Trail Talk by Bobby J. Copeland
Universal Horrors by Tom Weaver
Ultimate John Wayne Trivia Book
Ultimate Unauthorized Star Trek Quiz Book by Robert W. Bly
Valley of the Cliffhangers Supplement by Jack Mathis
The Vanishing Legion by John TuckaWest That Never Was by Tony Thomas
Wayne's World: Extreme Close-up by Mike Myers and Robin Ruzan
Way Out West by Jane and Michael Stern
Western Films of John Ford by J. A. Place
Whatever Happened to Randolph Scott? by C. H. Scott
Who Is That? by Warren B. Meyers
Wizard of Oz: The Official 50th Anniversary Pictorial History by John Fricke, Jay Scarfone, and William Stillman
Words and Shadows by Jim Hitt

For complete book list with prices, write to: Empire Publishing, Inc., Box 717, Madison, NC 27025-0717

INDEX

Acuff, Roy, 17, 91, 99, 127
Armstrong, Louie, 101
Arnold, Jimmy, 9
Autry, Gene, 131
Baker, Kenny, 9, 51, 79
Bean Blossom, 9, 11, 25, 47, 59, 73
Bluegrass Cardinals, 49
Boxcar Willie, 89
Boys from Shiloh, 57
Bradley, Owen, 87
Bryan, James, 51
Burch, "Junior" Curtis, 17
Burns, George, 125
Bush, Gene, 63
Bush, Sam, 17
Butler, Carl, 97. 109
Butler, Pearl, 97
Campbell, Archie, 91
Campers, 25
Carson, Martha, 95
Carter, June, 85, 131
Carter, Maybelle, 129
Cash, Johnny, 101, 123
Clements, Vassar, 71
Cline, Curly Ray, 35, 75
Cline, Patsy, 127
Collie, Biff, 95
Cooke, Jack, 35
Cooper, Wilma Lee, 77, 85
Connell, Dudley, 53
Davis, Hubert, 63
Davis, Jimmie, 127
Davis, John, 49
Davis, Ruby, 63
Davis, Shelby-Jean, 63
Davis, Skeeter, 85
Dickens, Little Jimmy, 129
Douglas, Jerry, 15
Drake, Pete, 97
Durham, Buddy, 95

Fesler, Brian, 57
Flatt and Scruggs, cover, 13, 27, 45
Flatt, Lester, cover, 13, 27, 33, 45, 55, 65
Ford, Tennessee Ernie, 131
Forrester, Howdy, 9
Gimble, Johnny, 115
Goldsboro, Bobby 131
Graves, Josh, cover
Green, Joe, 9
Haggard, Merle, 115
Harkreader, Sid, 119
Harrell, Bill, 77
Harris, Doc, 9
Harris, Emmylou, 81
Hartford, John, 73, 117
Hartgrove, Mike, 81
Hee Haw, 91
Hester, "Hoot," 75
Hicks, Bobby, 75
Hoffman, Richard, 63
Howard, Jan, 85
Jarrell, Tommy, 9
Jeralds, Wayne, 57
Jim and Jesse, 11, 55
Johnson, Johnny, 55
Johnson Mountain Boys, 53
Jones, Grandpa, 81, 91
Jones, Ramona, 117
Kershaw, Doug, 111
Krauss, Alison, 69
Lee, Ricky, 31
Lee, Roy, 31
Lewis Family, 61
Lindsey, George "Goober," 91
Lonzo and Oscar, 111
Lyle, Frances, 131
Lynn, Loretta, 125
Magaha, Mac, 105
Maphis, Joe, 95
Maphis, Rose Lee, 95

Martin, Grady, 97
Martin, Jimmy, 39
Martin, Jimmy, Jr., 39
Minnie Pearl, 85, 99
Monroe, Bill, 21, 29, 41, 51, 59, 67, 73
Moss, Frazier, 117
McCormick, George, 105
McLain Family, 23
McLaughlin, David, 53
McMahon, Ed, 131
Nikirk, Doyle, 57
O'Bryant, Alan, 37, 81
Osborne Brothers, 65
Oswald, Bashful Brother, 133
Parker, Rex and Eleanor, 95
Parmley, Don, 49
Paul, "Woody," 125
Phillips, Stu, 109
Pruett, Jeanne, 99
Reno, Don, 19, 77
Riddle, Jimmy, 127
Riley, Jeannie C., 131
Ritter, Tex, 131, 133
Roberts, H. G., 127
Roberts, Kenny, 95
Robbin, Larry, 53
Roman, Lulu, 91
Russell, Johnny, 93
Ryan, Buck, 19
Samples, Junior, 91
Samson, Darrel, 39
Samson, Sheridon, 39
Sanders, Colonel, 67
Scruggs, Earl, cover, 13, 27, 45, 69
Seckler, Curly, 27
Shepard, Jean, 129
Skaggs, Ricky, 35, 75
Smathers, Ben, 99, 113
Smiley, Red, 19

Smith, Billy, 81
Smith, Bobby, 57
Smith, Dallas, 57
Smith, Kenneth, 57
Smith, Terry, 77, 81
Smith, Tim 49
Snow, Hank, 107, 121
Spradlin, Tim, 39
Stanley, Ralph, 31, 35
Stoney Mountain Cloggers, 113
Stubbs, Eddie, 53
Stuart, Joe, 79
Stuart, Marty, 65
Sullivan, Dad, 71
Sullivan, Oscar, 111
Terry, Gordon, 115
Thompson, Hank, 103
Travis, Merle, 91, 95
Trent, Buck, 105
Tubb, Ernest, 109
Tullock, "Cousin" Jake, cover, 45
Twitty, Conway, 87
Underwood, Richard, 53
Wagoner, Porter, 105, 121
Walker, Cindy, 107
Walker, Ebo, 17
Walmsley, Jon, 89
Warren, Paul, cover, 27, 45, 55, 65
Watson, Doc, 43, 73
Wells, Kitty, 85, 103
Wheeler, Onie, 127
White, Roland, 55
Whites, The, 15
Whitley, Keith, 35
Wiseman, Mac, 37
Wood, Del, 93
Wooten, David (Lonzo), 111
Wright, Johnny, 103
Wright, Norman, 49